For Shannon

Text copyright © 2018 by Vivian French
Illustrations copyright © 2018 by Catherine Rayner

First U.S. edition 2018

Library of Congress Catalog Card Number pending
ISBN 978-1-5362-0167-3

CCP 23 22 21 20 19 18
10 9 8 7 6 5 4 3 2 1

Printed in Shenzhen, Guangdong, China

This book was typeset in Godlike.
The illustrations were done in mixed media.

Candlewick Press
99 Dover Street
Somerville, Massachusetts 02144

visit us at www.candlewick.com

CANDLEWICK PRESS

Hello, Horse

Vivian French

illustrated by

Catherine Rayner

I HAVE a friend named Catherine, and she has a horse named Shannon.

"Come and meet her," Catherine says.

I'm not sure if I like horses.

"Shannon likes people,"
Catherine tells me.
"And you'll like Shannon."

She points to a horse eating
grass by the fence.

"There she is."

"She's SO big," I say.

"Shannon may be big compared to you, but she's very kind," says Catherine. Then she calls, "Shannon! I've brought someone to meet you!"

A horse's height is measured from the withers (a point between its shoulders) to the ground. Shannon is 15.2 hands (5 feet 2 inches, or about 154 centimeters) high.

Shannon throws her head up
to look at us as we walk over
to meet her. I stare at her.

She's beautiful!
Her eyes are dark, and she
looks as if she knows
everything there is to know.

Horses' eyes are on either side of their heads, which
means they can see almost all the way around.

Catherine pulls a carrot out of
her pocket and breaks it in half.

"Here. Keep your hand very flat so that she doesn't nibble your fingers by mistake. She won't mean to, but she can't tell where your fingers end and the carrot begins."

I hold out my hand, and Shannon takes the carrot. Her mouth feels like soft velvet.

Horses are herbivores, which means they eat plants.

"She's got VERY tickly whiskers!" I say,
and Shannon pulls her head back as if she's shocked.

"Horses have sensitive hearing."
Catherine rubs Shannon's nose.
"You have to talk quietly to
them. Would you like to
lead her to the yard?"

I feel proud leading Shannon across the field.

The ground is hard, and her feet

CLIP-CLOP as we go.

"Her feet are very noisy," I say.

"She's wearing metal shoes," Catherine explains.

"They protect her hooves."

Horses' hooves are like our fingernails—
they keep growing and need regular trimming.

When we get to the other side of the field, Catherine ties Shannon's rope to the fence. There's a bucket full of brushes, and I watch as Catherine chooses one.

"What are you doing?" I ask.

"I'm going to groom her. When I've brushed off all the mud and dust, we'll put on her saddle and bridle, and you can go for a ride."

"Oh." I look at Shannon.
She puts her head down
and looks at me.

Grooming is not only to keep the horse clean; it's a good way to check for cuts or injuries.

19

FWOOOOF! She puffs at me through her nostrils. I feel her breath on my face, and it makes me laugh. "There," says Catherine. "She likes you! You can blow back . . . very gently. Then she'll know you like her too."

Humans have lived and worked with horses for thousands of years.

All the time we're talking,
Catherine is brushing Shannon, and I can
tell that Shannon enjoys it. Even her legs get
brushed! I'd feel funny if someone brushed mine.

"All done," says Catherine, and she goes to get the saddle and bridle.

"Um," I say, and I look at my feet. "I'm not sure I want . . ."

Catherine doesn't hear me. She puts on Shannon's saddle and bridle, and then she pulls a big strap tight. "We're almost ready," she says.

I don't say anything.

"Now," says Catherine, "time
for your first ride. Put
your foot in the stirrup."
My tummy has
butterflies, but
I do as she says.

"Take hold of the reins. You can hold
her mane if you feel wobbly!" Then
Catherine takes my other foot, and—

25

"OH!" I say.
I'm sitting on
Shannon's back,
and it's very high up . . .

*It's important to always wear
a helmet, in case you fall off.*

and Shannon makes a funny little whickering noise.
It's as if she's saying, "Well done."

And I'm riding.

Now I have a friend named Shannon,
and Shannon has a new friend . . .

me.

AUTHOR'S NOTE

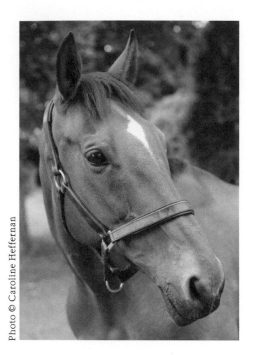

When I was little I loved horses, and I still do. Although I did think they were very big and a little bit scary!

Catherine is a real person (she's the illustrator of this book!) and Shannon is her horse. They've known each other for more than twenty years, so Shannon is very special to Catherine. I met Shannon quite a while ago and we became friends, too . . . and that's what gave me and Catherine the idea for *Hello, Horse.*

People have been making friends with horses for thousands of years. And just like people, horses each have their own ideas about things and their own ways of behaving. Catherine says Shannon is loyal, ticklish, and sometimes pretends to be grumpy, especially when she has to come in from the field. She's always very kind to children, though. Perhaps she knows that some of them are a little bit anxious!

INDEX

Look up the pages to find out about all these horse things. Don't forget to look at both kinds of word — **this kind** and *this kind*.

MORE INFORMATION

If you'd like to know more about horse care, try Colin Vogel's *Complete Horse Care Manual* (Dorling Kindersley, 2011).

These tools are especially useful for grooming:

body brush

hoof pick

dandy brush

mane and tail comb